BASS BUILDERS

SIMPLIFIED
SIGHT-READING FOR BASS
FROM THE FUNDAMENTALS TO THE ENTIRE FINGERBOARD

by Josquin des Pres

Audio Access Included

T0048229

To access audio visit:
www.halleonard.com/mylibrary

Enter Code
3683-9132-7643-5061

Cover photography by Pete Demos / CARVIN

ISBN 978-0-7935-6518-9

HAL•LEONARD®
CORPORATION
7777 W. BLUEMOUND RD. P.O. BOX 13819 MILWAUKEE, WI 53213

Visit Hal Leonard Online at
www.halleonard.com

SIMPLIFIED
SIGHT-READING FOR BASS
FROM THE FUNDAMENTALS TO THE ENTIRE FINGERBOARD

by Josquin des Pres

TABLE OF CONTENTS

Introduction

The ability to read music can be one of your most important assets in playing bass or any instrument. Besides opening new doors for working situations, it provides you with a better understanding of music fundamentals and your role as an instrumentalist. Just as reading the words of a foreign language helps you make more sense of it, reading a musical phrase immediately clarifies how it sounds.

Simplified Sight Reading concentrates on rhythms and phrasings most commonly heard through decades of bass playing. You'll begin to learn what you need to know, not everything there is to know. This book also places a strong emphasis on reading rhythms because good rhythm reading skills are as important for a bass player as they are for a drummer.

Although *Simplified Sight Reading* provides some music fundamentals, if you are a beginner you may want to supplement your studies with a basic bass method. To maintain and further your reading skills when you are finished with this book, get your hands and eyes on any piece of bass music you can find.

About the Author

Josquin des Pres is a studio bass player, producer, songwriter, and author. His credits range from recording with such world class players as Alex Acuna, Jeff Porcaro, Steve Lukather, and Vinnie Colaiuta, to co-writing numerous songs with Elton John's lyricist, Bernie Taupin.

Acknowledgments

Special thanks to Carvin, Vigier, ART, La Bella, Monster Inc. cables, Lace Sensor pickups, and Marshank Group for their contribution to the audio recording.

Recorded and mixed at Continental Circus Audio.

Mastered by Scott Gorham.

How to Get the Most Out of This Book

Here are some very important rules to remember every time you practice:

Always use the accompanying audio tracks. They will make your reading studies more efficient and enjoyable. The track number appears next to each recorded example. Before picking up your instrument, listen and read the example you are about to study. Once you are familiar with its contents, use your instrument to play it. Adjust your own balance between metronome and bass. (The metronome click is on the left side of the stereo mix, and the bass is on the right side.) Use Track ◄1► to tune your instrument (G, D, A, E, high to low).

Always use a metronome, starting at 50 beats per minute. Tap your foot to each metronome click.

Always sing or hum every note you are playing. This will help you develop your ear. Good reading skills go hand in hand with a good ear.

Always try to read ahead, approaching groups of notes as if you were reading words. Avoid the common "spelling" method of reading rhythms, particularly when dealing with sixteenth notes (i.e., 1–e–and–a, 2–e–and–a, 3–e–and–a, 4–e–and–a). Instead, when you see ♫♩ think of it as "ta taa ta," for example. Also, ♩♫ = "taa ta ta," ♫♩ = "ta ta taa," ♫ = "taa taa," ♬ = "ta ta ta ta," and so on. With this method, you will identify rhythms much faster.

Chapter 1: Reading Fundamentals

Staff and Clef

A music staff has five lines and four spaces.
Bass music is written in bass clef.

Bass clef

Measures and Bar Lines

Measures divide music into small sections.
Bar lines separate measures.
The end of a large sections (e.g., verse, chorus, bridge, etc.) is marked by a double bar.

Measure   Bar lines   Double bar

Time Signatures

The most common time signature in popular music is $\frac{4}{4}$.
In this case, the top number indicates there are four beats, or counts, per measure.
The bottom number indicates each quarter note receives one count.

Note Duration

The shape of a note indicates its duration.
Some notes are hollow, some have stems, and some have stems with flags.

stems   flags

| Whole note | Half note | Quarter note | Eighth note | Sixteenth note |
| (4 beats) | (2 beats) | (1 beat) | (1/2 beat) | (1/4 beat) |

Consecutive eighth notes are connected by their flags to make them easier to read.

Consecutive sixteenth notes are also connected by their flags to make them easier to read.

Rests

Each note has an equivalent in silence called a rest.
Do not play for the duration of a rest.

| Whole rest
(4 beats) | Half rest
(2 beats) | Quarter rest
(1 beat) | Eighth rest
(1/2 beat) | Sixteenth rest
(1/4 beat) |

Pitch

The position of notes on the staff indicates their pitch.
The higher a note's pitch, the higher its position on the staff.
Ledger lines are used to expand the range of the staff.

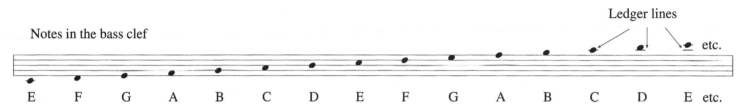

Chapter 2: Rhythms

The first step to good sight-reading is understanding rhythm. The exercises in this chapter focus exclusively on rhythms—from the very simple to the very complex. Each example should be played on a single D note (A string, fifth fret).

Play each exercise with a metronome. Let each beat (one metronome click or foot tap) equal one quarter note.

Tap your foot *down* on each beat:

Bring your foot *up* on each offbeat:

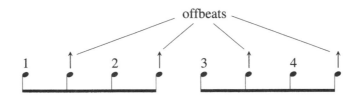

Simple Notes

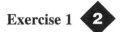

Whole note   Half note   Quarter note

Exercise 1

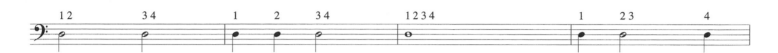

Exercise 1A

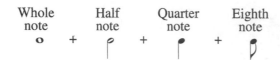

Exercise 2 ◆3

Exercise 2A

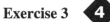

Whole note		Half note		Quarter note		Eighth note		Sixteenth note
o	+	♩	+	♩	+	♪	+	♪

Exercise 3

Exercise 3A

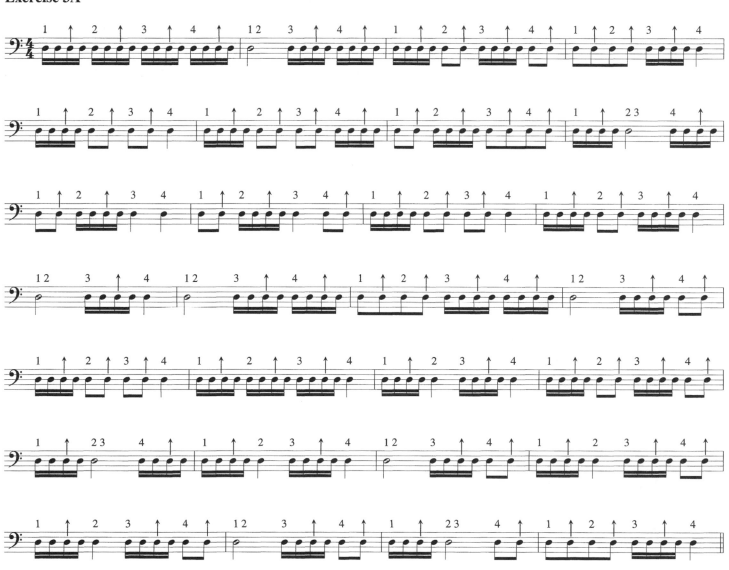

Simple Notes and Rests

Whole note		Half note		Quarter note		Whole rest		Half rest		Quarter rest
o	+	𝅗𝅥	+	♩	+	▬	+	▬	+	𝄽

Exercise 4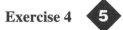

Exercise 4A

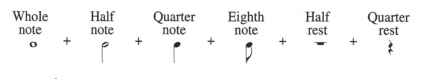

Exercise 5

Exercise 5A

13

Exercise 6

Exercise 6A

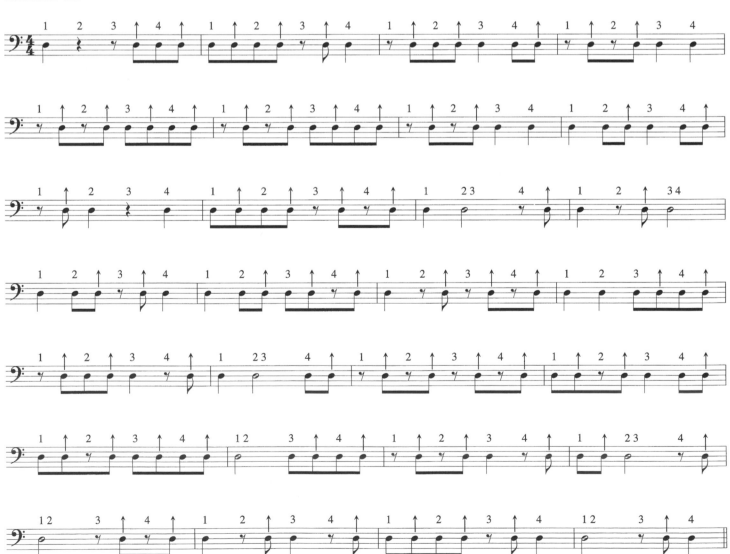

Combining Eighths and Sixteenths

Exercise 7

Exercise 7A

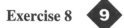

Exercise 8 ◆9◆

Exercise 8A

Combining Eighths and Sixteenths with Rests

Exercise 9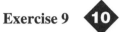

Exercise 9A

Exercise 10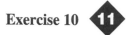

Exercise 10A

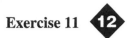

Exercise 11

Exercise 11A

Recapitulation

Exercise 12

Exercise 12A

The Dot

A dot added to a note or a rest increases its value by one half.

Half note (2 beats)	Dotted half note (3 beats)	Half rest (2 beats)	Dotted half rest (3 beats)
Quarter note (1 beat)	Dotted quarter note (1 1/2 beats)	Quarter rest (1 beat)	Dotted quarter rest (1 1/2 beats)
Eigth note (1/2 beat)	Dotted eighth note (3/4 beat)	Eigth rest (1/2 beat)	Dotted eighth rest (3/4 beat)

Exercise 13

Exercise 13A

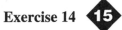

Exercise 14

Exercise 14A

 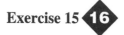

Exercise 15A

The Tie

A tie is used to create a note duration no single note can create by itself. Ties are also used to extend a note over a bar line into the next measure.

Don't pluck this note

Hold for the duration of one half note plus a sixteenth.

Don't pluck this note

Hold for the duration of a half note.

 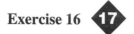

Exercise 16A

 **18**

Exercise 17A

27

A triplet is a group of *three* notes or rests performed in the time normally taken by just *two* notes or rests of the same value. Because there is an "extra" note involved in a triplet, each note is actually slightly shorter than its face value. For example, each note in a quarter note triplet is slightly shorter than a regular quarter note.

It is important when playing a triplet to remember each note in the triplet should receive equal time value. Whatever beat value you're playing within, try to *feel it,* or subdivde it, in three—rather than typical quarter, eighth, or sixteenth note subdivisions.

The Quarter Note Triplet

A quarter note triplet is a series of three quarter notes (or rests) of equal value that occur inside a half note group.

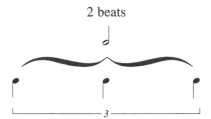

The Eighth Note Triplet

An eighth note triplet is a series of three eighth notes (or rests) of equal value that occur inside a quarter note group.

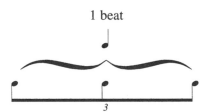

The Sixteenth Note Triplet

An sixteenth note triplet is a series of three sixteenth notes (or rests) of equal value that occur within an eighth note group.

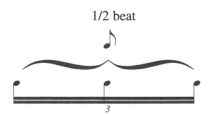

Exercise 18 ⟨19⟩

Exercise 18A

Exercise 19

Exercise 19A

Exercise 20

Exercise 20A

Exercise 21

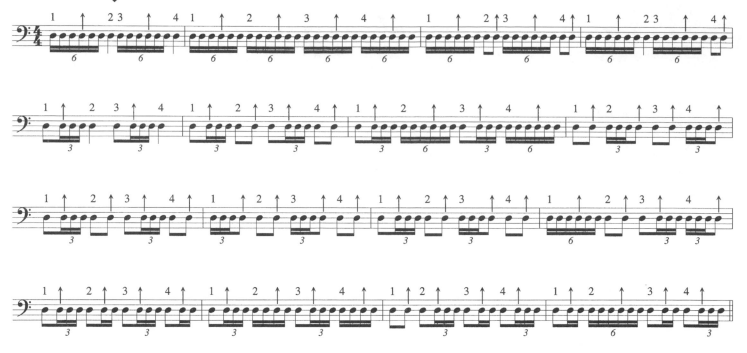

Exercise 21A

Exercise 22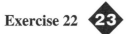

Exercise 22A

Exercise 23

Exercise 23A

Recapitulation

Exercise 24

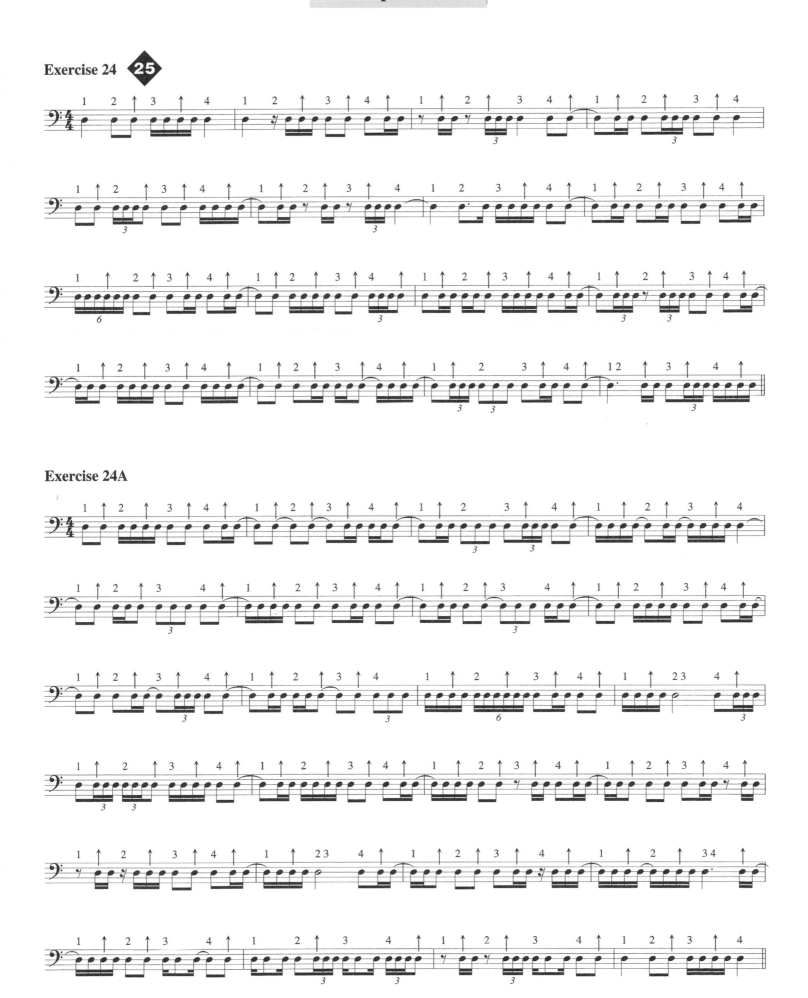

Exercise 24A

35

Chapter 3: Rhythms and Pitches

Let's simplify the rhythms and focus on the other crucial aspect of sight-reading—pitch. The chart below illustrates the basic open position notes for bass.

Notes on the E string

Notes on the A string

Notes on the D string

Notes on the G string

To keep things manageable, the following sets of exercises begin with notes on a single string—the low E—and then progressively expand to include notes on the A string, the D string, and finally the G string.

Refer back to the above chart if you find yourself having difficulty with any of the notes.

Notes on the E String

Exercise 1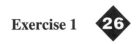

Exercise 1A

Exercise 2   **27**

L.H. fingering

4 2 4 0 4 2   4 4 0 1   4 0 4 4 0 2 4   4 0 1 2 4 0

2 4 2 4 1 4 0   4 1 4 0 2 4   2 0   2 4 4 2 1 2 4 0

4 0 1 2 0 0   4 2 4 1 4 0   4 1 4 1 4 0   4 1 4 2 4 0

Exercise 2A

Notes on the E and A Strings

Exercise 3

Exercise 4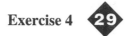

L.H.
fingering

Exercise 4A

Notes on the E, A, and D Strings

Exercise 5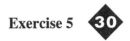

Exercise 5A

Exercise 6 31

L.H.   2   4   4   4 2 1 2 2   1   2 2 4   4   4 1 4 1 0   4 4
fingering

4   2 2 1   4 4   1   1 2 4 1 2   2 2 1   4 4 4 2 1   1 4 4

0 1 1 2 4   2   4 2 2   1   4 1 1 4 1   4 2 4   4 1 4   4

4 2 1   0   0 4 2 1 2   1   4 4 2 2 1   1 2 2 4 1

Exercise 6A

Notes on the E, A, D, and G Strings

Exercise 7

Exercise 8

L.H.
fingering

Exercise 8A

Studies on All Four Strings

Exercise 9—Without Rests

Exercise 9A

Exercise 10—With Rests

Exercise 10A

Chapter 4: Intervals

Thirds

A space to the next space above equals a third (major or minor).

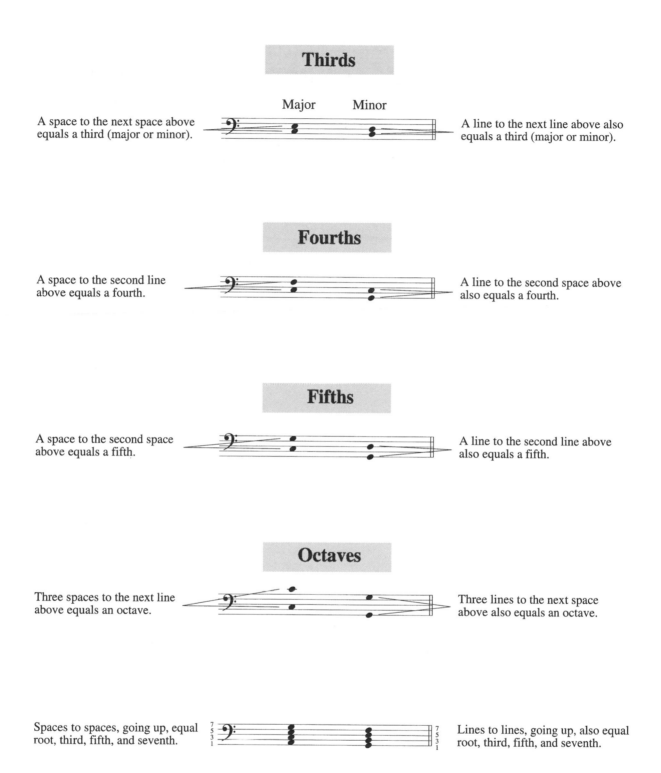

A line to the next line above also equals a third (major or minor).

Fourths

A space to the second line above equals a fourth.

A line to the second space above also equals a fourth.

Fifths

A space to the second space above equals a fifth.

A line to the second line above also equals a fifth.

Octaves

Three spaces to the next line above equals an octave.

Three lines to the next space above also equals an octave.

Spaces to spaces, going up, equal root, third, fifth, and seventh.

Lines to lines, going up, also equal root, third, fifth, and seventh.

Being aware of the intervals you are playing is another aspect of effective sight-reading. The following exercises focus on the most common intervals in bass music—thirds, fourths, fifths, and octaves.

Thirds

Each measure contains four intervals of a third, grouped in pairs.

Exercise 1

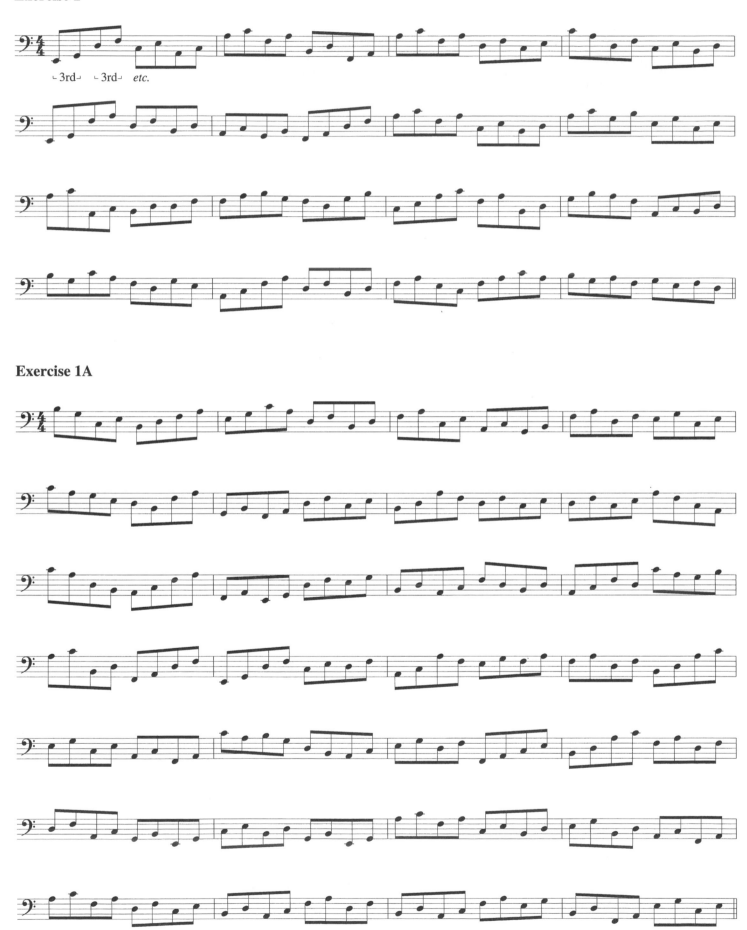

Exercise 1A

Fourths

Each measure contains four intervals of a fourth grouped in pairs.

Exercise 2

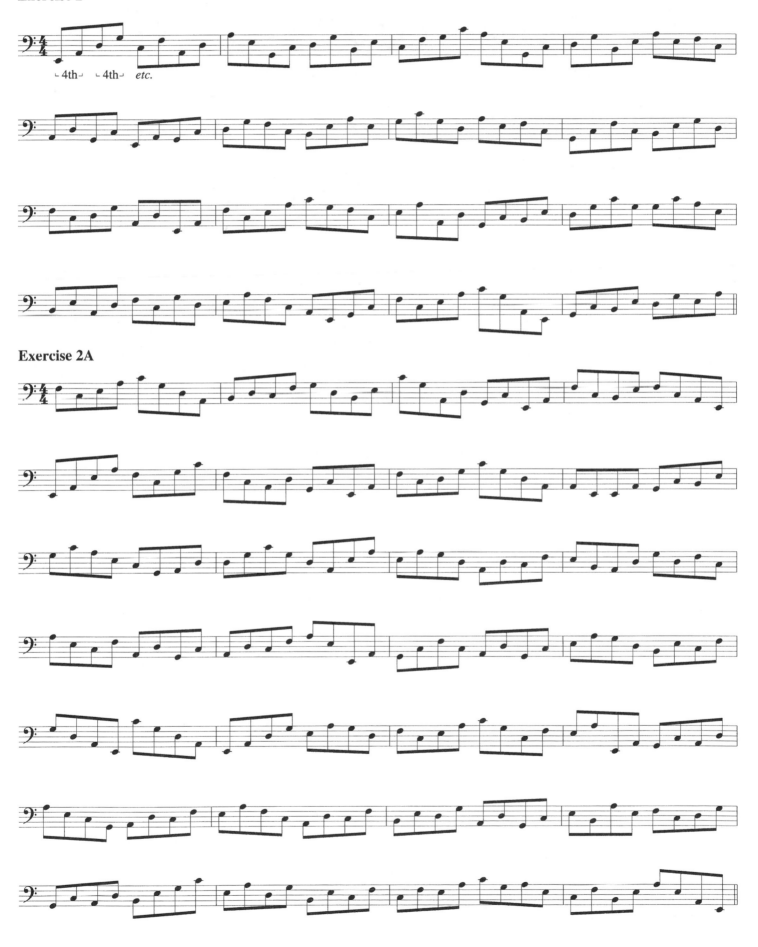

Exercise 2A

Fifths

Each measure contains four intervals of a fifth grouped in pairs.

Exercise 3

└5th┘ └5th┘ *etc.*

Octaves

Each measure contains four intervals of an octave grouped in pairs.

Exercise 4

└oct.┘ └oct.┘ *etc.*

Chapter 5: Accidentals

An accidental is a sign used to raise or lower a note by one half step.

Sharp (♯)
The sharp sign raises a note by one half step.
Move the note one fret up to the next adjacent fret.

Flat (♭)
The flat sign lowers a note by one half step.
Move the note down to the next adjacent fret.

Natural (♮)
The natural sign cancels a previous sharp or flat.
Play the note as is.

Accidentals remain in force for the whole measure in which they appear—unless cancelled by a natural. Sometimes, naturals are used in the measure immediately following an accidental, as a courtesy reminder that a sharp or flat is no longer in effect.

Whole Notes with Sharps and Flats

Exercise 1

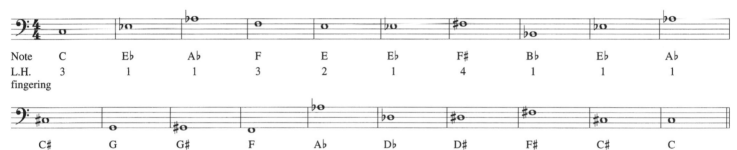

Note	C	E♭	A♭	F	E	E♭	F♯	B♭	E♭	A♭
L.H. fingering	3	1	1	3	2	1	4	1	1	1

C♯	G	G♯	F	A♭	D♭	D♯	F♯	C♯	C
4	3	4	1	1	4	1	4	4	3

Exercise 2

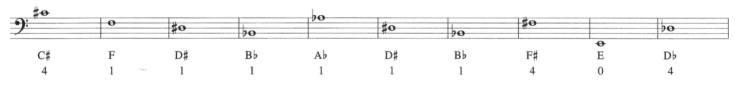

C♯	F	D♯	B♭	A♭	D♯	B♭	F♯	E	D♭
4	1	1	1	1	1	1	4	0	4

G♯	A♭	D♯	G♯	E	D♭	F	F♯	B♭	C
1	1	1	4	1	4	2	4	2	1

Half Notes with Sharps and Flats

Exercise 3

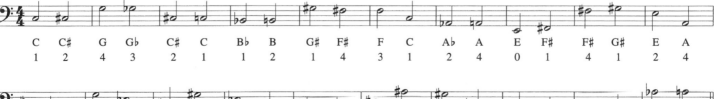

C	C♯	G	G♭	C♯	C	B♭	B	G♯	F♯	F	C	A♭	A	E	F♯	F♯	G♯	E	A
1	2	4	3	2	1	1	2	1	4	3	1	2	4	0	1	4	1	2	4

D♯	D	G	E♭	C♯	G♯	E♭	A♭	F	F♯	D♯	A♯	G♯	B♭	A♯	F♯	E	G♭	A♭	A
1	4	4	1	4	1	1	4	1	2	1	4	1	1	1	2	0	2	1	2

Quarter Notes with Sharps and Flats

Exercise 4

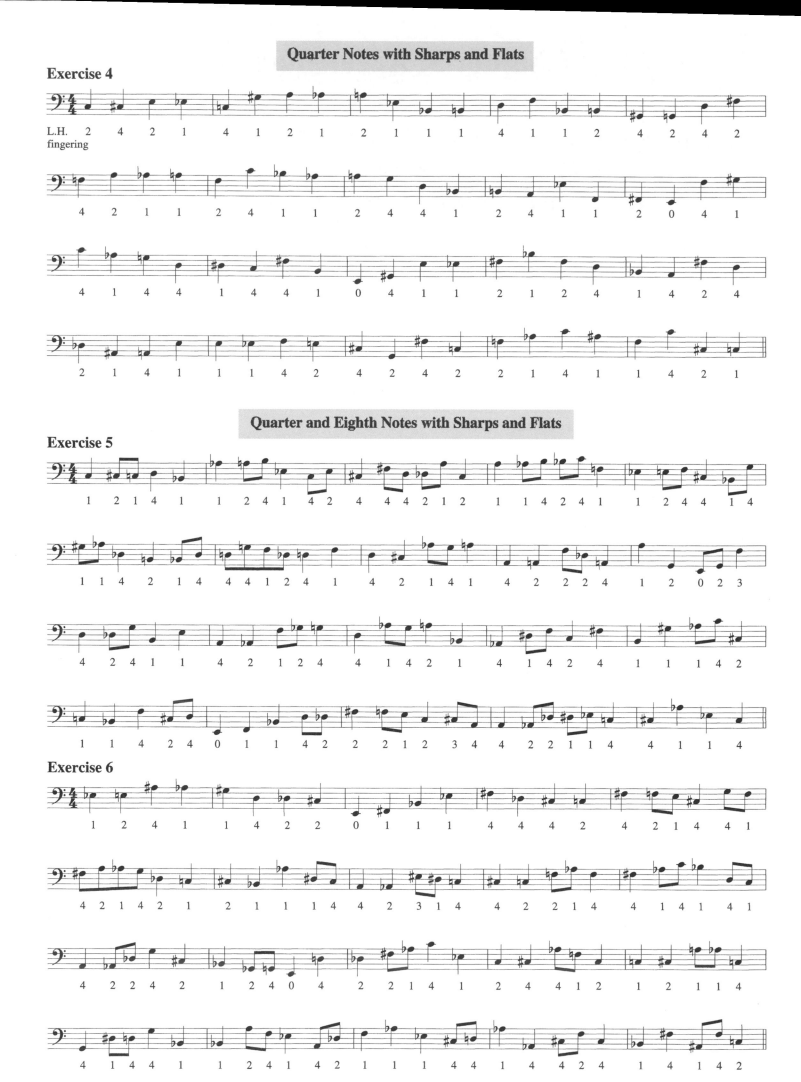

Quarter and Eighth Notes with Sharps and Flats

Exercise 5

Exercise 6

When two note names refer to the same pitch (e.g., C♯ and D♭), those notes are called enharmonic equivalents. While a typical piece of music normally uses just one of those note names, this last exercise uses both—to give you practice in recognizing enharmonic equivalents and in reading a single pitch in two ways.

Remember enharmonic equivalents refer to the exact same pitch and therefore require no change in fingering.

Recapitulation: Enharmonic Equivalents

Exercise 7

Chapter 6: Key Signatures

When you are reading a new piece of music, the first thing to do is to take notice of the key signature, then practice up and down the scale in that particular signature. This will help both your ears and your hands get familiar with the notes of that key.

The following is a table of the most common major and minor key signatures and their corresponding scales.

Major Keys

Minor Keys

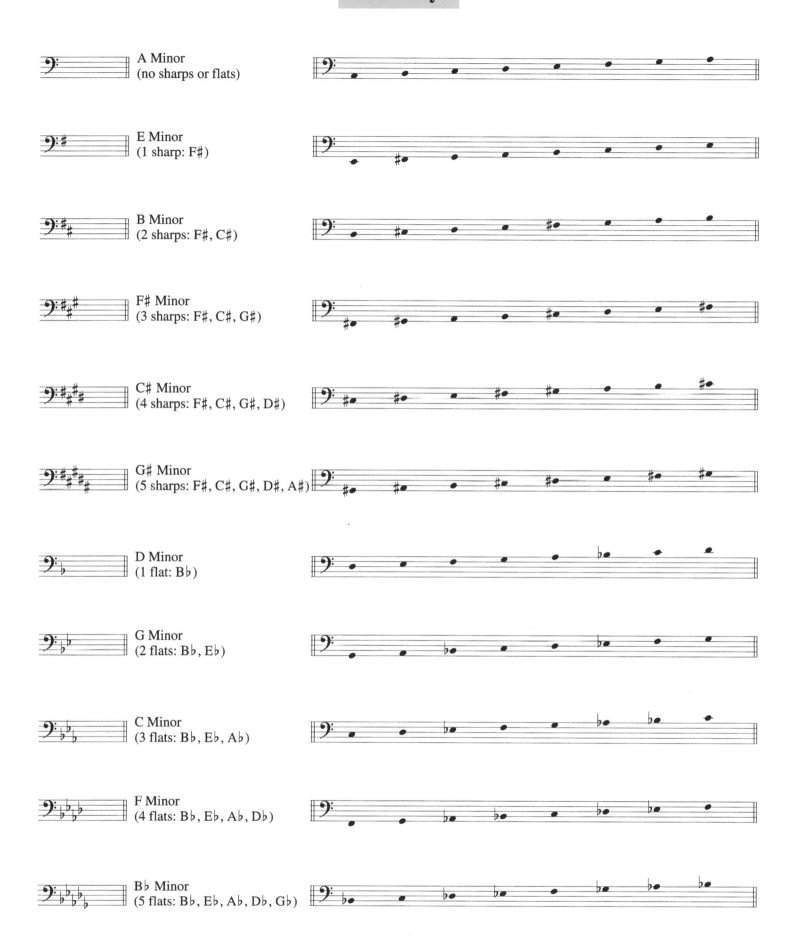

If you encounter a piece of music with no indicated key signature, it means either the music is in the key of C major, A minor, or a related mode, or it has no specific key and the accidentals will be written in as they occur.

Major Keys

These exercises incorporate rhythms commonly found in all styles of popular music. Remember to note the key signature of each exercise and to play up and down the appropriate scale before starting.

If you have questions about the fingering of any of the higher notes here, refer to the Bass Fingerboard Chart on page 60.

Exercise 1—C Major (No sharps or flats) 36

Exercise 2—G Major (1 sharp: F♯) 37

Exercise 3—D Major (2 sharps: F♯, C♯) 38

Exercise 4—A Major (3 sharps: F♯, C♯, G♯) 39

Exercise 5—E Major (4 sharps: F♯, C♯, G♯, D♯) 40

Exercise 6—B Major (5 sharps: F♯, C♯, G♯, D♯, A♯) 41

Exercise 7—F Major (1 flat: B♭)

Exercise 8—B♭ Major (2 flats: B♭, E♭)

Exercise 9—E♭ Major (3 flats: B♭, E♭, A♭)

Exercise 10—A♭ Major (4 flats: B♭, E♭, A♭, D♭)

Exercise 11—D♭ Major (5 flats: B♭, E♭, A♭, D♭, G♭)

Minor Keys

Exercise 12—A Minor (No sharps or flats) 47

Exercise 13—E Minor (1 sharp: F♯) 48

Exercise 14—B Minor (2 sharps: F♯, C♯) 49

Exercise 15—F♯ Minor (3 sharps: F♯, C♯, G♯) 50

Exercise 16—C♯ Minor (4 sharps: F♯, C♯, G♯, D♯) 51

Exercise 17—G♯ Minor (5 sharps: F♯, C♯, G♯, D♯, A♯) 52

Exercise 18—D Minor (1 flat: B♭) 53

Exercise 19—G Minor (2 flats: B♭, E♭) 54

Exercise 20—C Minor (3 flats: B♭, E♭, A♭) 55

Exercise 21—F Minor (4 flats: B♭, E♭, A♭, D♭) 56

Exercise 22—B♭ Minor (5 flats: B♭, E♭, A♭, D♭, G♭) 57

Chapter 7: The Entire Fingerboard

Bass Fingerboard Chart

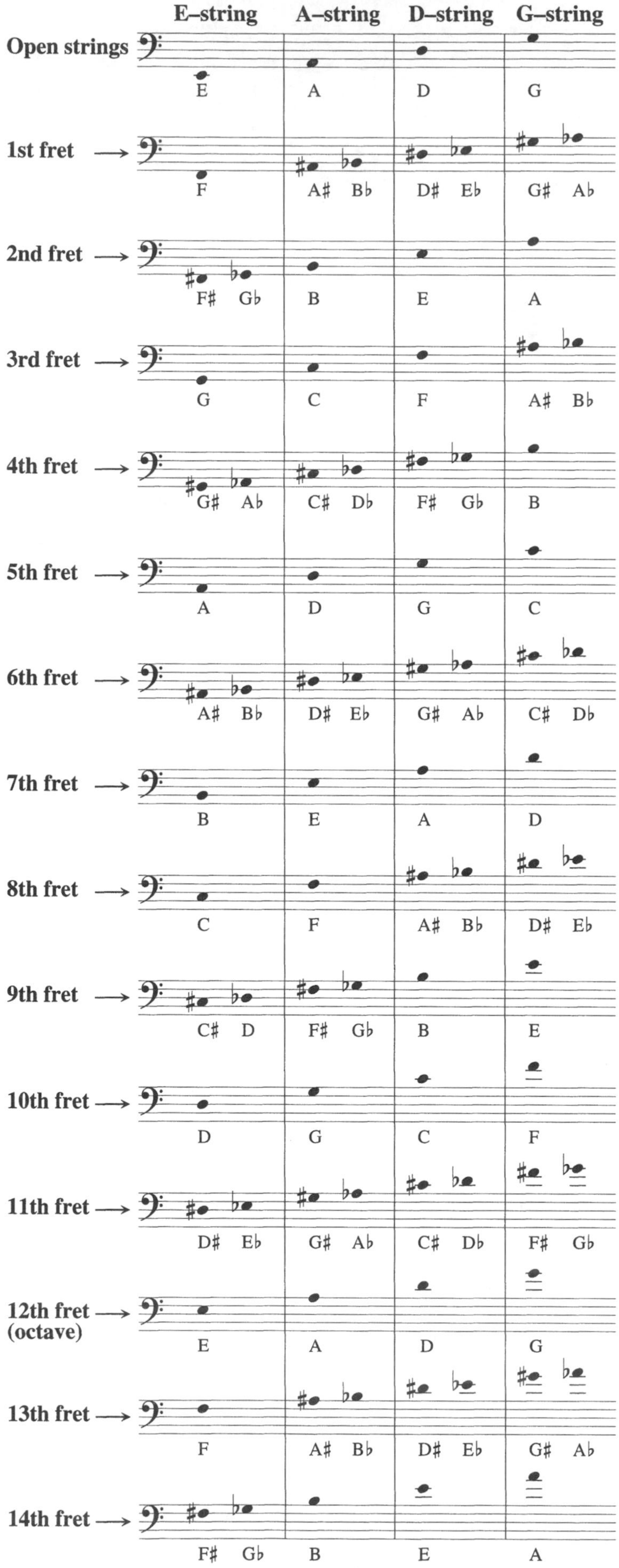

Major Scales

Close study of these two-octave scales will help you unlock the upper register of the bass fingerboard and increase your fluency in the major and minor keys just covered.

Exercise 1—C Major

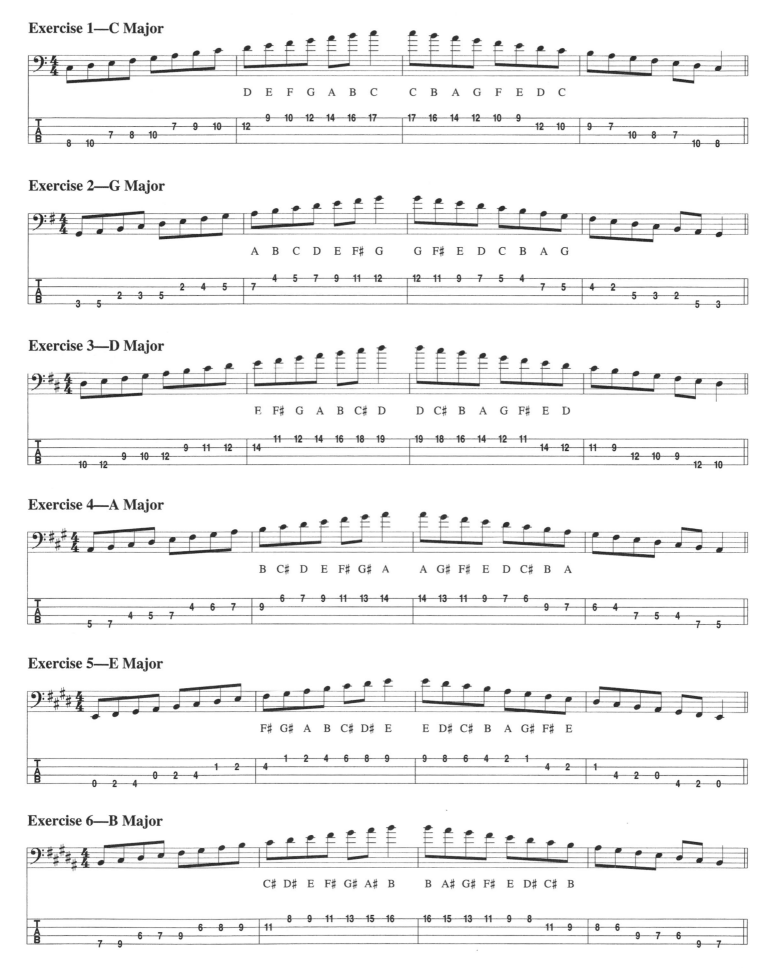

Exercise 2—G Major

Exercise 3—D Major

Exercise 4—A Major

Exercise 5—E Major

Exercise 6—B Major

Exercise 7—F Major

G A Bb C D E F   F E D C Bb A G F

Exercise 8—Bb Major

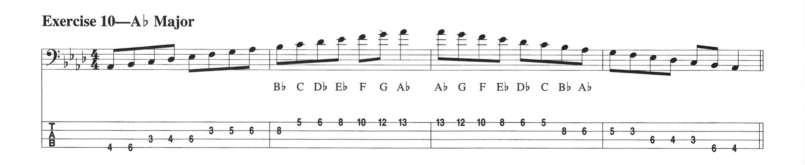

C D E F G A Bb   Bb A G F E D C Bb

Exercise 9—Eb Major

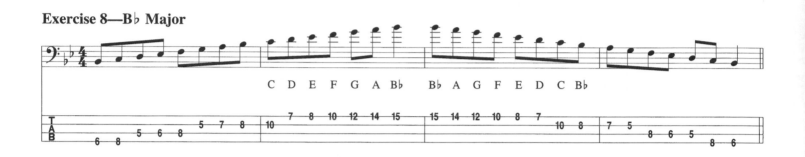

F G Ab Bb C D Eb   Eb D C Bb Ab G F Eb

Exercise 10—Ab Major

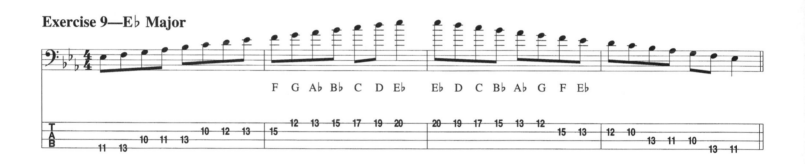

Bb C Db Eb F G Ab   Ab G F Eb Db C Bb Ab

Exercise 11—Db Major

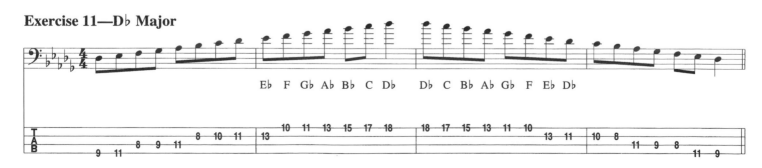

Eb F Gb Ab Bb C Db   Db C Bb Ab Gb F Eb Db

Minor Scales

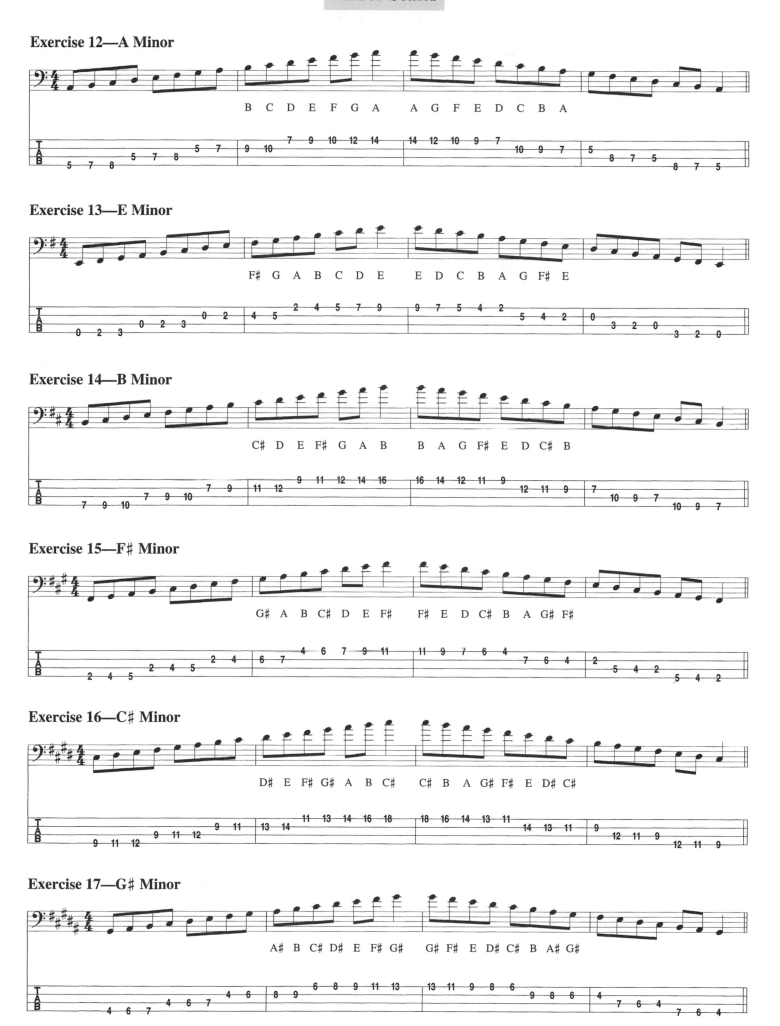

Exercise 12—A Minor

B C D E F G A A G F E D C B A

Exercise 13—E Minor

F♯ G A B C D E E D C B A G F♯ E

Exercise 14—B Minor

C♯ D E F♯ G A B B A G F♯ E D C♯ B

Exercise 15—F♯ Minor

G♯ A B C♯ D E F♯ F♯ E D C♯ B A G♯ F♯

Exercise 16—C♯ Minor

D♯ E F♯ G♯ A B C♯ C♯ B A G♯ F♯ E D♯ C♯

Exercise 17—G♯ Minor

A♯ B C♯ D♯ E F♯ G♯ G♯ F♯ E D♯ C♯ B A♯ G♯

Exercise 18—D Minor

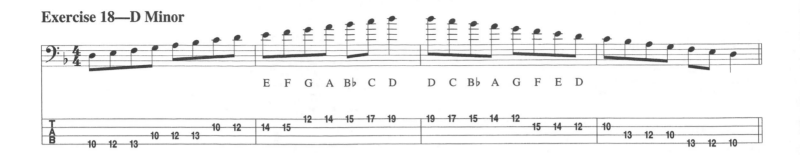

E F G A Bb C D   D C Bb A G F E D

Exercise 19—G Minor

A Bb C D Eb F G   G F Eb D C Bb A G

Exercise 20—C Minor

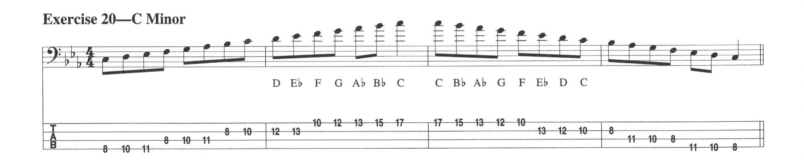

D Eb F G Ab Bb C   C Bb Ab G F Eb D C

Exercise 21—F Minor

G Ab Bb C Db Eb F   F Eb Db C Bb Ab G F

Exercise 22—Bb Minor

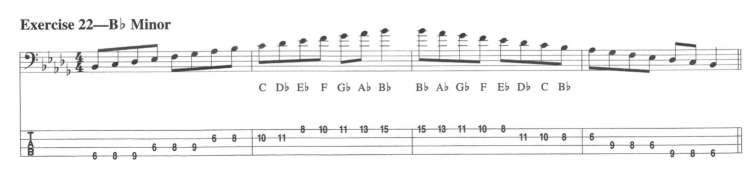

C Db Eb F Gb Ab Bb   Bb Ab Gb F Eb Db C Bb

Chapter 8: Bass Patterns and Styles

Now is the time to use your photographic memory! The exercises in this chapter represent bass patterns heard in all styles of music, through decades of bass playing. Repeat each pattern several times until you are familiar with its contents—rhythms, notes, intervals, and key signatures. Memorize not only the sound of each pattern, but the way it looks as well.

Becoming familiar with a variety of common bass patterns such as these will give you a jump start the next time you try to read a new piece of music or come up with an accompaniment to a new tune.

Remember: Always use a metronome, sing or hum every note you play, and never let your eyes off of the paper!

Blues

R&B/Funk

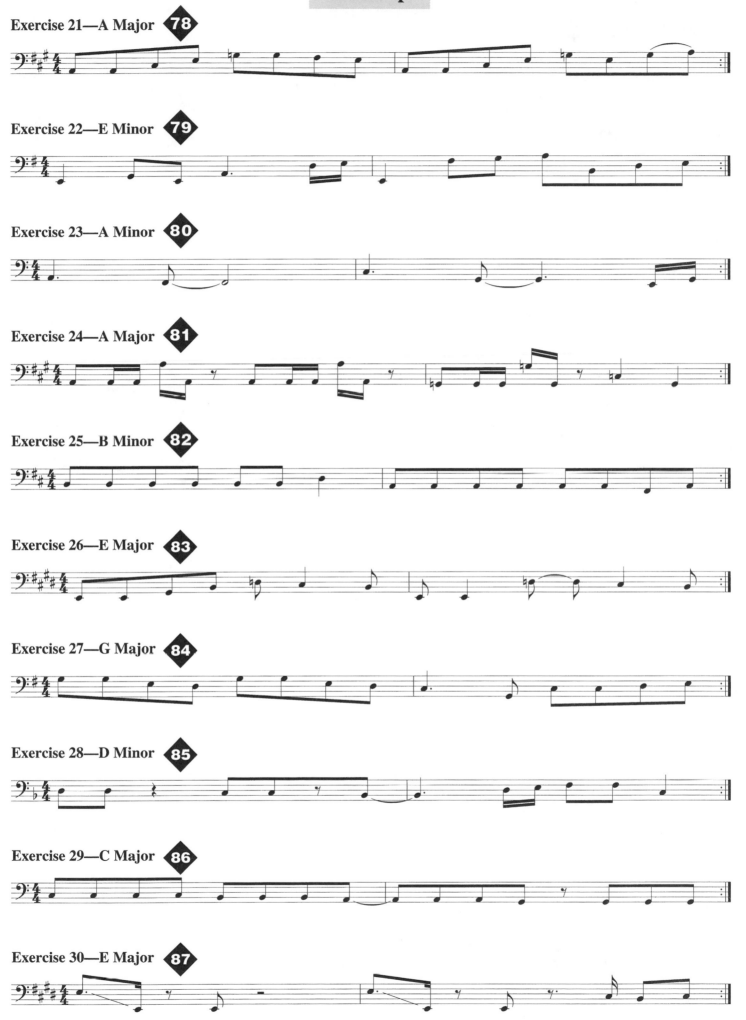

Latin

Exercise 31–C Major 88

Exercise 32–A Major 89

Exercise 33–D Major 90

Exercise 34–A Minor 91

Exercise 35–G Major 92

Exercise 36–G Minor 93

Exercise 37–F Major 94

Exercise 38–C Major 95

Exercise 39–A Major 96

Exercise 40–B♭ Major 97

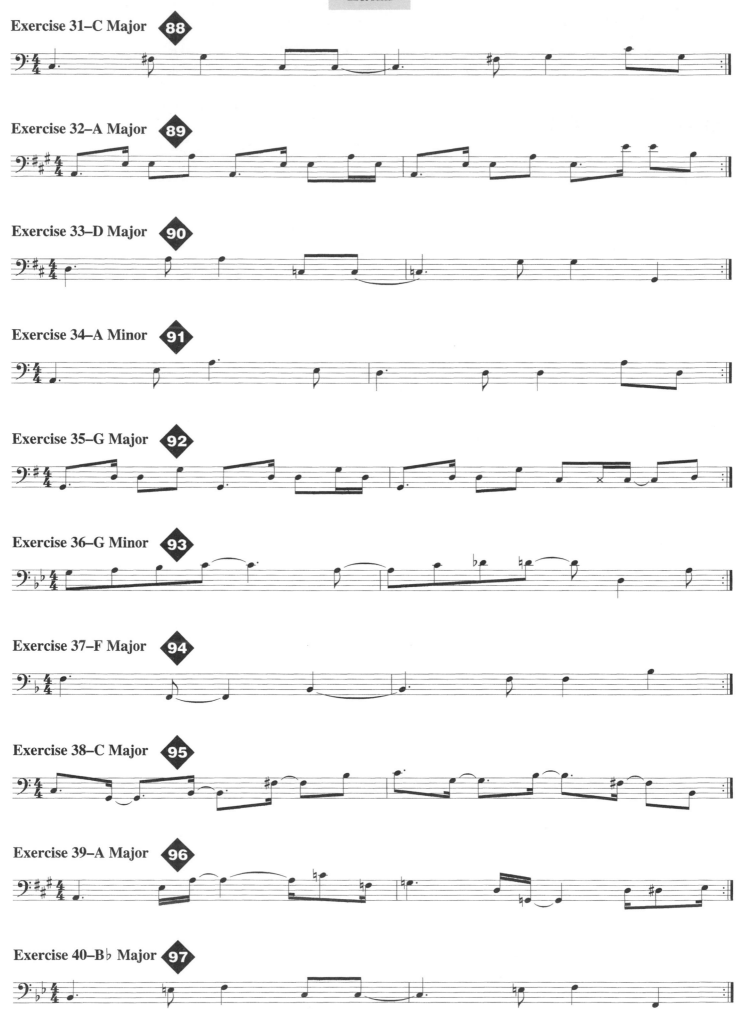

Glossary of Music Terms and Symbols

Understanding the signs, symbols, and terms of music can be every bit as important as being able to read the notes. Failure to notice or understand these symbols is a common weakness among all readers. Before you start figuring out the notes to a piece, make sure you notice the other signs that tell you what's going on.

The following is a list of the most common terms and symbols to watch out for:

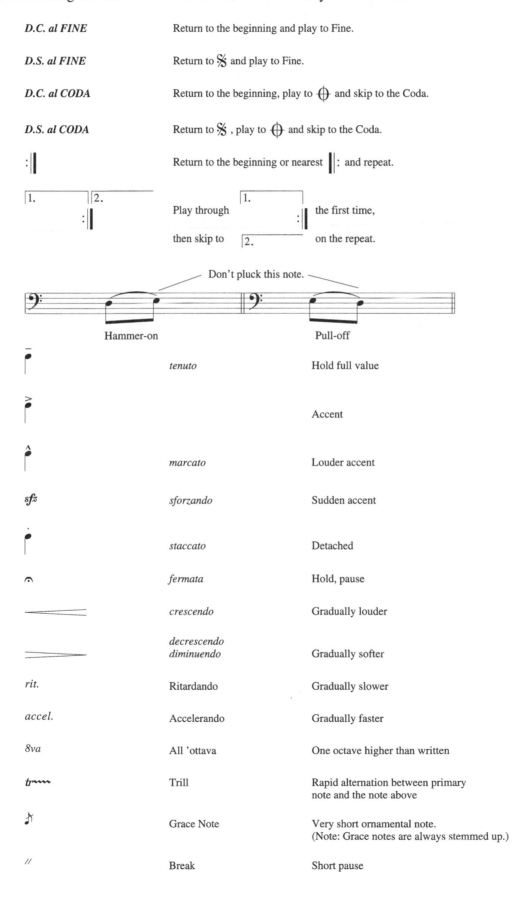

D.C. al FINE		Return to the beginning and play to Fine.
D.S. al FINE		Return to 𝄋 and play to Fine.
D.C. al CODA		Return to the beginning, play to ⊕ and skip to the Coda.
D.S. al CODA		Return to 𝄋, play to ⊕ and skip to the Coda.

Return to the beginning or nearest ‖: and repeat.

Play through [1. the first time, then skip to 2. on the repeat.

Don't pluck this note.

Hammer-on   Pull-off

	tenuto	Hold full value
		Accent
	marcato	Louder accent
sfz	*sforzando*	Sudden accent
	staccato	Detached
	fermata	Hold, pause
	crescendo	Gradually louder
	decrescendo *diminuendo*	Gradually softer
rit.	Ritardando	Gradually slower
accel.	Accelerando	Gradually faster
8va	All 'ottava	One octave higher than written
tr〜〜	Trill	Rapid alternation between primary note and the note above
♪	Grace Note	Very short ornamental note. (Note: Grace notes are always stemmed up.)
//	Break	Short pause

BASS BUILDERS

A series of technique book/audio packages created for the purposeful building and development of your chops. Each volume is written by an expert in that particular technique. And with the inclusion of audio, the added dimension of hearing exactly how to play particular grooves and techniques make these truly like private lessons.

BASS FOR BEGINNERS
by Glenn Letsch
00695099 Book/CD Pack........................$19.95

BASS GROOVES
by Jon Liebman
00696028 Book/Online Audio $19.99

BASS IMPROVISATION
by Ed Friedland
00695164 Book/Online Audio $19.99

BLUES BASS
by Jon Liebman
00695235 Book/Online Audio $19.99

BUILDING WALKING BASS LINES
by Ed Friedland
00695008 Book/Online Audio $19.99

**RON CARTER –
BUILDING JAZZ BASS LINES**
00841240 Book/Online Audio $19.99

DICTIONARY OF BASS GROOVES
by Sean Malone
00695266 Book/Online Audio $14.95

EXPANDING WALKING BASS LINES
by Ed Friedland
00695026 Book/Online Audio $19.99

FINGERBOARD HARMONY FOR BASS
by Gary Willis
00695043 Book/Online Audio $17.99

FUNK BASS
by Jon Liebman
00699348 Book/Online Audio $19.99

FUNK/FUSION BASS
by Jon Liebman
00696553 Book/Online Audio $24.99

HIP-HOP BASS
by Josquin des Prés
00695589 Book/Online Audio $15.99

JAZZ BASS
by Ed Friedland
00695084 Book/Online Audio $17.99

**JERRY JEMMOTT –
BLUES AND RHYTHM &
BLUES BASS TECHNIQUE**
00695176 Book/CD Pack........................$24.99

JUMP 'N' BLUES BASS
by Keith Rosier
00695292 Book/Online Audio $17.99

THE LOST ART OF COUNTRY BASS
by Keith Rosier
00695107 Book/Online Audio $19.99

PENTATONIC SCALES FOR BASS
by Ed Friedland
00696224 Book/Online Audio $19.99

REGGAE BASS
by Ed Friedland
00695163 Book/Online Audio $16.99

'70S FUNK & DISCO BASS
by Josquin des Prés
00695614 Book/Online Audio $16.99

**SIMPLIFIED SIGHT-READING
FOR BASS**
by Josquin des Prés
00695085 Book/Online Audio $17.99

6-STRING BASSICS
by David Gross
00695221 Book/Online Audio $14.99

HAL•LEONARD®

halleonard.com

Prices, contents and availability subject to change without notice; All prices are listed in U.S. funds